The Vegetable
Garden Cookbook

Oliver Brachat
Tobias Rauschenberger

The Vegetable
Garden Cookbook

60 Recipes to Enjoy Your Homegrown Produce

Skyhorse Publishing

Content

Dear Readers,

What could be lovelier than a stroll through a weekly farmers' market? The bold hues, the scents, the passage of the seasons revealed in the colorful stalls... Each time I am dazzled anew by the richness I encounter here. I can hardly wait for summer when the first sun-ripened eggplants are being sold. Or autumn, when the succulent pumpkins and squash are ready. Then there is winter with its crisp cabbage, and the few short weeks of spring when freshly harvested asparagus can be found everywhere.

As a child, I loved the fresh ingredients picked out of our own garden. I think fondly about how my mother bought fresh seeds every year to grow little seedlings that were later transferred to our vegetable garden. Diligence, a lot of sun, and plenty of water were the requirements for harvesting our own vegetables months later. How wonderful it is to use your own tomatoes for preparing scrumptious salads and aromatic sauces!

This enthusiasm for fresh vegetables is something Oliver Brachat and I would like to share with you. We want to inspire you to let vegetables play the leading roles to explore their full culinary ranges. Through carefully selected spices and creative preparation, you can use vegetables throughout the year as the basis for delicious and healthy meals. This book will hopefully provide you with a broad range of inspirations and ideas to help you in this endeavor. The alphabetical organization of vegetable types will enable you to quickly find just what you need. Please do not be confused by the different oven temperatures provided in the recipes; the first setting is always the recommended one. If your oven is not convection you can still cook all your meals with a conventional oven on the second temperature setting.

Now, take your time, grab your shopping basket, and let yourself be seduced by the exhilarating diversity of the market. Dive into the rich offerings of nature, and bring vegetables to the table! We hope you will have a wonderful time in the kitchen. Bon appetit!

Tobias Rauschenberger & Oliver Brachat

Eggplant

Eggplants come in a rich diversity of shapes and colors. When the fruit ripens, it is evenly colored and glossy.

With its origins in India, eggplants need a lot of sun and a very warm climate because they cannot tolerate frost. Therefore, it is a good idea to grow them in a greenhouse in colder regions.

Eggplant is a popular ingredient, especially in Mediterranean dishes like Ratatouille and Moussaka. Moreover, eggplant is ideal in the preparation of mouth-watering dips or for grilling. Sprinkling a little oil or citric acid on the pulp will prevent the brown discoloration.

Baked Eggplant Stuffed with Ground Lamb

4 small eggplants

Salt

Pepper

5 tablespoons olive oil

1¼ pounds (600 g) ground lamb

1 onion

1 clove of garlic

2 teaspoons cumin

½ teaspoon cinnamon

2 teaspoons paprika, spicy

5 sprigs of thyme

3 tomatoes

1 bunch of parsley

¾ cup + 1½ tablespoons
    (200 ml) vegetable broth

ALSO:

Roasting pan

Wash the eggplants, cut in half and remove the pulp with a spoon. Avoid perforating the skin. Use a knife to create a flat surface on the bottom of the eggplants, so that they will not tip over in the roasting pan. Sprinkle with a hearty pinch of salt and pepper. Mince the flesh of the eggplant and set aside. Heat 3 tablespoons of olive oil and fry the ground lamb until crumbly. Season with salt and pepper and transfer the lamb to a bowl. Dice the garlic and onion. Using the remaining olive oil in the same pan, lightly sauté for 3 minutes. Add to the browned lamb.

Preheat the convection oven to 320°F/160°C (for a conventional oven: 355°F/180°C). Season the ground lamb with cumin, cinnamon, and paprika. Rinse the thyme, blot dry, and pull the leaves off the stems. Wash the tomatoes, remove the cores, and dice. Wash the parsley, blot dry, and cut into small pieces. Stir the thyme, tomatoes, and parsley into the lamb mixture.

Dab the inside of the eggplants dry with paper towels, fill with the lamb mixture, and place the stuffed eggplants into the roasting pan. Pour vegetable broth into the pan and bake for 30 to 40 minutes.

Serve hot.

Makes 4 servings

Preparation time: ca. 45 minutes

Bake time: 30–40 minutes

Eggplant Chips

Wash the eggplants and cut off the stems and ends. Using a sharp knife or a food slicer, cut the eggplants into ¾- to 1-inch slices. Salt well and place in a colander so the eggplant slices can drip dry. Let sit for 1 hour.

Dry the slices with a paper towel. Dredge the eggplant slices in the flour, shaking off the excess. Heat the vegetable oil and bake the chips at 340–350°F / 170–175°C until crispy. Place on paper towels to drain and season with Fleur de Sel.

Tip: If you want an oriental flavor, use a little cumin and chili salt as well.

2 eggplants
Salt
¾ cup + ⅛ cup (100 g) of flour
½ cup (300 ml) of vegetable oil
Fleur de Sel (French sea salt)

Makes 4 servings
Preparation time: ca. 1 hour

Cauliflower

The most common cauliflower is the white floret variety, but it comes in other colors as well, such as violet, yellow, and green (Romanesco). In the garden, the plant needs substantial space to grow, so leave enough room between each seedling.

Cauliflower has two seasons, early summer and late fall. Once the florets are firm and fragrant, it is ready to be picked. Cauliflower tastes best when it is fresh. Usually it is served as a side dish, but it is suitable as a vegetarian main dish, in a soup, or as an au gratin dish. Cauliflower is a good source of Vitamin C and fiber. Stored in a refrigerator, cauliflower will stay fresh for two to four days.

Pureed Cauliflower with Argan Oil

Wash the cauliflower and coarsely chop. Boil for 10 minutes in salted water until soft. Drain and puree with butter. Add mace, chili flakes, cumin, salt, and pepper.

Serve warm with sliced fresh French bread and argan oil.

Tip: This fits nicely with grilled chicken breast.

1 cauliflower (ca. 600 g)
Salt
⅔ cup (150 g) butter
1 pinch of mace
½ teaspoon chili flakes
1½ teaspoon cumin
Pepper

ALSO:
1 French loaf
1 small bottle of argan oil

Makes 4 servings
Preparation time: ca. 20 minutes

Cauliflower Tempura with Anchovy Mayonnaise

FOR THE TEMPURA:

1 cauliflower (ca. 600 g)

4 cups (1 liter) sunflower oil

1 egg white

¼ teaspoon baking power

½ cup (60 g) flour

⅓ cup (50 g) corn starch

1 teaspoon salt

1 teaspoon turmeric

⅔ cup (150 ml) ice cold water

1 tablespoon sesame seeds

FOR THE MAYONNAISE:

2 egg yolks

1 tablespoon mustard

1 teaspoon salt

¾ cup (200 ml) olive oil

5 anchovies

1 tablespoon capers

2 tablespoons caper water

Pepper

2 tablespoons lemon juice

Cut cauliflower into small florets. Rinse briefly under cold water and allow to drain.

For the anchovy mayonnaise, mix egg yolks with mustard and salt. Slowly add olive oil in a thin stream, stirring constantly until the mayonnaise becomes a thick cream. Finely chop the anchovies and capers and add to the mayonnaise along with the caper water. Flavor the mayonnaise with pepper and lemon juice.

Heat the sunflower oil to 350°F / 175°C. For the tempura, mix the baking powder with the flour, corn starch, salt, and turmeric. In another bowl, lightly beat the egg white. Stir the water into the egg white, and add to the flour mixture. Stir everything together until just combined. Immediately dredge the cauliflower florets in the batter and sauté until crispy and golden brown. Sprinkle with the sesame seeds and serve with the mayonnaise.

Makes 4 servings

Preparation time: ca. 1 hour

Beans

Beans are classified by the way they grow, either on bushes or poles. While bush beans grow close to the ground, pole beans are the climbing varieties. Legumes come in countless forms and colors; white and green beans, kidney beans, needle and wax beans are just a few.

This multifaceted vegetable is great in soups and delicious salads, or as a side dish. Beans should be prepared within short time frames, otherwise they quickly go limp. Fresh beans can be recognized by their firm hulls, which break when bent. Besides being a good source of important nutrients, beans are especially high in protein. They should be cooked and never eaten raw because of a naturally occuring toxin (phasin) that is destroyed during cooking.

Osso Buco with Green Beans

1 garlic clove

8 veal shanks (each 250–300 g)

Salt, pepper

¾ cup + 1 tablespoon (100 g) flour

5 tablespoons olive oil

4 onions

1 cup (200 ml) white wine

2¼ cups (500 ml) veal stock

4 cups (500 g) green beans

1 small bunch of thyme

ALSO:

Roasting pan

Preheat a convection oven: 340°F/170°C (for a conventional oven: to 375°F/190°C). Mince the garlic and rub it on both sides of the veal shanks. Season with salt and pepper and dust with flour. Heat the olive oil and brown the veal for two minutes per side. Place the veal in the roasting pan and set aside the drippings.

Coarsely slice the onions and add to the drippings. Sauté for 5 minutes. Deglaze onions with white wine and reduce by half.

Add the onions to the veal stock and pour over the veal in the roasting pan. Cover and braise in the oven for 1 hour. Clean the beans and cut into pieces. Rinse the thyme, blot dry, and pick off the leaves. Add the beans and thyme to the roasting pan. Cover and braise for an additional 45 minutes. Uncover for the last 15 minutes.

Tip: If you prefer a thicker sauce, remove the shanks and add corn starch to the sauce. Polenta tastes especially good as a side dish.

Makes 4 servings

Preparation time: ca. 45 minutes

Bake time: 1¾ hours

Cutlets with Bean Salad and Mustard Vinaigrette

For the salad, clean the beans and boil for approximately 5 to 8 minutes until al dente. Drain and rinse with cold water. For the vinaigrette, dice the shallots. Combine shallots with mustard, red wine vinegar, olive oil, vegetable broth, salt, pepper, and sugar. Cut the beans into bite-sized pieces and add to the bowl. Rinse the savory, blot dry, remove the leaves from the stems, coarsely chop, and add to the bowl, tossing everything together.

Preheat the convection oven to 350°F/180°C (for conventional oven: 390°F/200°C). Season the cutlets with salt and pepper. Pour the flour and bread crumbs onto separate plates. Whisk the eggs. Dredge the cutlets in the flour and shake off the excess. Dip cutlets into the eggs and allow to drip a little. Dredge the cutlets in the bread crumbs, pressing lightly into the pork. Brown the cutlets in sunflower oil over medium heat for 2 to 3 minutes per side. Melt butter in the pan and place in the oven for about 8 minutes. Halfway through, turn the cutlets one time while in the oven. Serve with the bean salad.

FOR THE SALAD:

3¼ cups (600 g) bush beans

Salt

2 shallots

2 teaspoons medium-strength mustard

6 tablespoons red wine vinegar

4 tablespoons olive oil

¼ cup (50 ml) vegetable broth

1 small bunch of savory

FOR THE PORK:

4 pork cutlets (each 200 g)

Salt, pepper

¾ cup + 1 tablespoon (100 g) flour

2 cups + 3 tablespoons (200 g) bread crumbs

2 eggs

½ cup (150 ml) sunflower oil

1 tablespoon butter

Makes 4 servings

Preparation time: ca. 1 hour

Frying time: 10 minutes

Broccoli

Broccoli originally came from Asia Minor, and in Europe is predominately grown in Italy and France. Just like its cousin cauliflower, the broccoli's blossoms are consumed. However, the stems can also be delicious. When growing broccoli, make sure to water and fertilize the plants regularly. The vegetable is harvested in summer before the first buds open.

You can recognize fresh broccoli by its bright green color and unfurled blossoms. To reduce the cooking time and help retain broccoli's many vitamins, cut it into small florets. The vegetable tastes especially good with fish or meat.

Tortilla with Broccoli Cream and Smoked Salmon

Separate the broccoli florets from the stem and clean them. Boil until tender, approximately 10 minutes. Drain and rinse in cold water. Puree the broccoli with crème fraîche, cayenne pepper, and some salt.

Lightly toast tortillas on both sides in a hot pan. Wash, seed, and slice the tomatoes. Clean the romaine lettuce and tear the leaves into bite-sized pieces. Spread 1 to 2 tablespoons of broccoli cream onto the tortillas. Divide the tomatoes and lettuce between the tortillas. Add the smoked salmon.

Finely chop the pink peppercorns and sprinkle over the tortillas. Roll the tortillas up and enjoy.

ca. ½ head (300 g) broccoli
Salt
⅓ cup + 1 tablespoon (100 g) crème fraîche
¼ teaspoon cayenne
1 package of tortillas
3 tomatoes
2 romaine lettuce hearts
7 oz (200 g) smoked salmon
1 teaspoon pink peppercorns

Makes 4 servings
Preparation time: ca. 30 minutes

29

Broccoli Couscous with
Teriyaki Chicken Skewers

Rinse the chicken breasts in cold water and pat dry with paper towels. Cut the breasts into strips and mix with the teriyaki sauce. Cover and marinate for 1 to 2 hours in the refrigerator.

Remove the broccoli florets from the stem. Rinse briefly, and allow to drip dry. Finely chop the florets and sear with 2 tablespoons of olive oil for 8 to 10 minutes. The broccoli should brighten in color and produce a wonderful roasted aroma. Flavor with salt and pepper.

Pour the couscous into a bowl and mix with ras el hanout. Bring the vegetable broth to a boil and pour over the couscous. Allow the couscous to sit for 5 minutes and then fluff with a fork. Wash and dice the chili pepper. Toast the pine nuts. Add the chili pepper, pine nuts, and broccoli to the couscous, carefully stirring everything together.

Heat the remaining 3 tablespoons of olive oil in a pan. Skewer the chicken strips accordion-style onto the wooden skewers. Pan fry for 3 minutes per side. Add the rest of the teriyaki sauce and honey to the chicken and caramelize. Place the couscous on the plate and layer the skewers on top.

4 chicken breasts
   (180–200 g each)
10 tablespoons teriyaki sauce
1 bunch (500 g) broccoli
5 tablespoons olive oil
Salt, pepper
1½ cups (250 g) couscous
1 teaspoon ras el hanout
1¾ cups (400 ml) vegetable
   broth
1 chili pepper
⅓ cup (60 g) pine nuts
2 teaspoons honey

ALSO:
8 wooden skewers

Makes 4 servings
Preparation time: ca. 40 minutes
Marinating time: 1–2 hours

31

Broccoli Phyllo Tarts

1 bunch (500 g) broccoli

Salt

⅓ cup + 1 tablespoon (100 g)
   crème fraîche

1 onion

1 tablespoon olive oil

4 eggs

Pepper

Cayenne pepper

7 tablespoons (100 g) butter,
   melted

6 sheets of phyllo dough

2 tablespoons bread crumbs

2 cups (200 g) feta cheese

ALSO:

8" tart pan

Cut the broccoli florets from the stem and rinse under cold water. Boil for 10 minutes in salted water until tender. Drain and rinse in cold water. Place in a bowl and mix with the crème fraîche. Chop the onion and sauté in olive oil for 3 minutes until translucent. Cool and add to the broccoli mixture. Whisk the eggs and add to the broccoli mixture. Season well with salt, pepper, and cayenne. Stir thoroughly.

Preheat the convection oven to 340°F/170°C (for conventional oven: 375°F/190°C). Lay the phyllo dough sheets across the surface of the tart pan covering the edge of the pan. Coat each sheet well with melted butter. Sprinkle with bread crumbs and spread the broccoli mixture evenly. Crumble the feta across the mixture. Fold the dough edges over and brush with the remaining melted butter. Bake for 30 minutes. Allow to cool and serve.

For 8" tart pan

Preparation time: ca. 50 minutes

Bake time: 30 minutes

Mushrooms

Mushrooms were discovered in France in the seventeenth century and are available year round. There are both white and brown mushrooms, although the brown ones are stronger in flavor. One indicator of freshness is the closed gills under the cap.

Mushrooms are very sensitive, and should be handled carefully. When storing them, be sure to avoid direct sunlight and damp or warm storage. Raw mushrooms are an ideal addition to salads. Cooked mushrooms are particularly good paired with white meats, noodles, and rice. Besides that, they are the perfect basis for various sauces.

Creamy Mushroom
Soup with Meat Dumplings

FOR THE SOUP:

17½ oz (500 g) brown mushrooms

2 shallots

1 garlic clove

2 tablespoons butter

⅓ cup + 2 teaspoons (90 ml)
   chicken broth

1¼ cup (300 ml) cream

3 tablespoons + teaspoon
   (50 ml) cognac

Salt, pepper

3 green onions

FOR THE DUMPLINGS:

11 oz (300 g) ground boar

3½ oz (100 g) pork neck

1 stale roll

⅓ cup + 4 teaspoons (100 ml)
   lukewarm milk

1 small onion

1 tablespoon butter

1 egg

¼ teaspoon game spice mix

Salt, pepper

4 tablespoons olive oil

For the soup, clean the mushrooms, slicing 4 small ones and setting them aside. Dice the shallots and garlic. Heat the butter and sauté the whole mushrooms for 5 minutes. Add the shallots and garlic, cooking briefly. Pour in the chicken broth and cream, and simmer for 20 minutes. Add the cognac and season with salt and pepper. With an immersion mixer, puree the soup. If you prefer, pour the soup through a sieve.

For the dumplings, run the ground boar and pork neck through the finest setting of a meat grinder. Cube the roll and soften the pieces in the milk. Dice the onion and sauté in butter until translucent. Place the prepared ingredients into a bowl, and add the egg, wild game spice mix, salt, and pepper. Mix well. With damp hands, form the small dumplings and fry in 3 tablespoons of olive oil, turning frequently. Remove the dumplings and set the pan to a side.

Clean and chop the green onions. Sauté briefly with the mushroom slices in the remaining olive oil. Divide between the soup bowls and then fill with the soup.

Makes 4 servings

Preparation time: ca. 40 minutes

Cook time: ca. 20 minutes

Giant Stuffed Mushrooms

15 giant mushrooms

4 tomatoes

Salt

2 onions

1 garlic clove

2 tablespoons olive oil

17½ oz (180 g) smoked ham

1 small bunch of parsley

½ cup (60 g) parmesan cheese

¾ cup + 4 teaspoons (200 ml)
 vegetable broth

ALSO:

Roasting pan

Clean the giant mushrooms and remove the stems. Wash the tomatoes and cut shallow crosses into the bottoms. Remove the cores. Blanch the tomatoes in salted water for 15 to 20 seconds. Drain and immediately rinse in cold water. Remove the skin and seeds and cut into cubes.

Dice the onions and garlic. Cut 3 mushrooms into small cubes and sauté in the olive oil for 2 minutes. Add the onion and garlic and briefly cook together. Spoon the mixture into a bowl. Cut the ham into small pieces. Rinse the parsley, blot dry, and remove and chop the leaves. Add the tomatoes and parsley to the mushroom mixture.

Preheat the convection oven to 340°F/170°C (for conventional oven: 375°F/190°C). Fill the remaining twelve mushrooms with the mixture, pressing lightly into the hollowed centers. Finely grate the parmesan cheese and sprinkle on the mushrooms. Place the mushrooms into the roasting pan and pour the vegetable broth over them. Braise in the oven for 30 minutes.

Makes 4 servings

Preparation time: ca. 40 minutes

Bake time: 30 minutes

Peas

Peas were first cultivated over 4,000 years ago in China and are one of the oldest crops in the world. Today this popular legume is cultivated worldwide. While there are numerous varieties, the most well-known are round or shelling peas, wrinkled peas, and snow peas. The season for legumes runs from June through the end of September. The plants do not thrive in extreme damp conditions, and they require climbing aids. Besides being set out in beds, peas can also be grown in pots.

Peas are available in an array of forms: fresh, frozen, or canned. However, they taste best fresh out of the garden. The protein- and vitamin-rich legumes are excellently suited for purees, stews, or side dishes. You can retain their glowing colors by adding sugar to the cooking water or rinsing them in cold water immediately after cooking.

Pea Soup with Cream and Bacon

FOR THE SOUP:
1 onion
1 tablespoon olive oil
17½ oz (500 g peas), shelled
⅓ cup + 4 teaspoons (100 ml)
    Noilly Prat (vermouth)
3⅓ cups (800 ml) chicken broth
¾ cup + 4 teaspoons (200 ml)
    cream
Salt, pepper, freshly grated
    nutmeg

FOR THE CREAM AND BACON
    MIXTURE:
1 shallot
2 tablespoons olive oil
2 oz (60 g) streaky bacon
⅓ cup + 4 teaspoons (100 ml)
    milk
⅓ cup + 4 teaspoons (100 ml)
    cream
Salt
Pepper

ALSO:
8 strips of bacon
Baking parchment

Makes 4 servings
Preparation time: ca. 30 minutes
Cook time: ca. 15 minutes
Bake time: 12 minutes

For the soup, dice the onion and sauté in olive oil until translucent. Add the peas and cook for 5 minutes. Deglaze with the Noilly Prat and reduce by half. Add the chicken broth and simmer for 10 minutes. Then add the cream, blending everything well with an immersion mixer. Season the soup with salt, pepper, and nutmeg.

For the cream and bacon mixture, preheat the convection oven to 350°F/180°C (for conventional oven: 390°F/200°C). Place the bacon slices onto a baking sheet lined with baking parchment. Bake for 10 to 12 minutes until crispy. Dice the shallot. Chop bacon into cubes and render in olive oil. Add the shallot and sauté briefly. Add the milk and cream and simmer for 5 minutes. Pour through a sieve and flavor with salt and pepper.

Serve the pea soup in deep soup bowls. Froth the bacon sauce with a milk frother or an immersion mixer and add a dollop of frothy sauce to the soup. Serve with the crispy strips of bacon.

Pasta with Peas and Prosciutto

Dice the onion and garlic. Tear the prosciutto into small pieces. Heat the olive oil and butter and lightly sauté the the onion, garlic, and prosciutto for 5 minutes. Deglaze with the Noilly Prat and almost fully reduce. Add the cream and peas, and simmer for 5 minutes.

For the pasta, boil the pasta in salted water until al dente. Drain and reserve a ladle-full of the salted water to add to the pasta sauce. Immediately mix the hot penne with the sauce. Rinse the chives, blot dry, and chop. Gently fold into the penne and sauce. Season with pepper.

1 onion
1 garlic clove
5 oz (150 g) prosciutto, cut in slices
2 tablespoons olive oil
1 tablespoon butter
⅓ cup + 4 teaspoons (100 ml) Noilly Prat (vermouth)
1 cup + 2 teaspoons (250 g) cream
9 oz (250 g) peas, shelled
Salt
4¾ cups (500 g) penne
1 bunch of chives
Pepper

Makes 4 servings
Preparation time: ca. 20 minutes

45

Pea Cream with Toasted Bread

1 baguette

5 tablespoons olive oil

10½ oz (300 g) fresh peas,
    shelled

Salt

Pepper

¼ teaspoon Espelette pepper

2 tablespoons sour cream

3 sprigs of mint

Preheat the convection oven to 320°F/160°C (for conventional oven: 350°F/180°C). Cut the baguette into very thin, angled slices. Sprinkle with olive oil and roast for 10 to 12 minutes in the oven. Allow to cool.

Blanch the peas for 5 minutes in salted water. Drain and rinse with cold water. Set aside to drain fully. Rinse and blot dry the mint leaves. Combine the peas, mint, salt, pepper, Espelette pepper, and sour cream. Serve the pea cream with toasted bread.

Makes 4 servings

Preparation time: ca. 20 minutes

Bake time: 12 minutes

Fennel

Known as a healing plant because of its positive effect on digestion, fennel belongs to the celery family. Cultivated biennially, fennel comes in several varieties including spice and vegetable fennel, as well as wild fennel. Although the wild kinds are undemanding, vegetable fennel requires nutrient-rich soil and a warm, sunny location in the bed.

Fresh fennel has juicy, green foliage and a firm white to light green base, which can be enjoyed either raw or cooked. Fennel tastes delicious as a vegetable side dish for fish and makes heavier meat dishes more digestible. Fennel seeds are excellent as spices and are found in fennel tea and honey. Fennel stays good for several days in the refrigerator.

Fennel Soup with a Cheese Sandwich

1 tablespoon butter, melted
1 onion
1 garlic clove
7 oz (200 g) floury potatoes
½ cup + 2 tablespoons (150 ml) white wine
3⅔ cups (850 g) chicken broth
21 oz (600 g) fennel
½ cup + 1 tablespoon (150 g) crème fraîche
Freshly grated nutmeg
Black pepper
3 tablespoons Pernod

ALSO:
5 oz (150 g) nicely aged Gouda
8 pieces of very thin crisp bread

Chop the onion and garlic and sauté for 5 minutes in the butter. Peel and cube the potatoes, and add to the onion mixture. Sauté briefly, and deglaze with the white wine. Reduce somewhat and add the vegetable broth.

Wash the fennel, separating the leaves and setting aside. Remove the stem and coarsely chop the fennel. Add to the soup, cover, and simmer for 20 minutes.

Preheat the convection oven to 320°F/160°C (for conventional oven: 350°F/180°C). Coarsely grate the Gouda, dividing it between four slices of crisp bread. Set the remaining slices of bread on top of the cheese and bake for 10 minutes. Turn off the oven and keep the sandwiches warm.

Add the crème fraîche to the soup. Flavor the mixture with nutmeg, pepper, and Pernod. With an immersion mixer, blend the soup well and if desired, strain it through a sieve. Chop the fennel leaves and use as a garnish for the soup. Serve the sandwiches warm with the soup.

Makes 4 servings
Preparation time: ca. 40 minutes
Cook time: ca. 20 minutes
Bake time: 10 minutes

Orange Fennel Salad
and Turkey Steaks

FOR THE SALAD:

4 fennel heads

Fleur de Sel, pepper

1 lemon

3 oranges

2 tablespoons honey

4 tablespoons olive oil

FOR THE STEAKS:

4 turkey steaks (each 6 oz [160 g])

Salt

Pepper

2 teaspoons coriander

2 tablespoons olive oil

For the salad, wash the fennel heads, cut in half, and gore out the stems. With either a grater or a knife, slice the fennel into very thin pieces. Place these in a bowl and season them with Fleur de Sol and pepper. Squeeze the juice from the lemon and add to the fennel. Mix well and let stand for 15 minutes. Slice two of the oranges, remove the peel, and carefully cut the slices free. Squeeze out all of the remaining juice, along with the juice of the last orange. Simmer and reduce by half. Add the honey to the juice.

Drain the water off the fennel and marinade it with the orange sauce and olive oil. Fold in the orange slices.

For the steaks, season the turkey with salt and pepper. Coarsely chop the coriander seeds and sprinkle on the steaks. Brown the steaks in olive oil for 3 minutes per side, turning frequently. Divide the salad between the plates and serve with the steaks.

Makes 4 servings

Preparation time: ca. 40 minutes

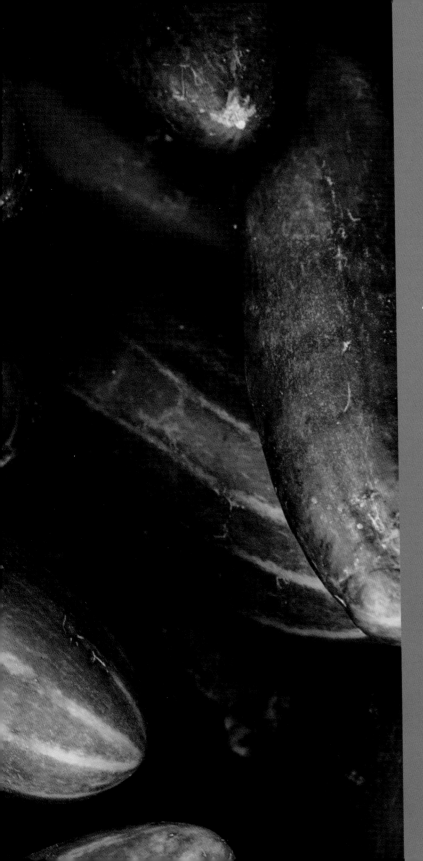

Cucumbers

Cucumbers belong to the squash family and are quite sensitive because they cannot tolerate frost. Therefore they cannot be transferred from pots to outdoor beds any earlier than late May. The simplest way is to grow them in a greenhouse. Cucumbers need a significant amount of water and nutrient-rich soil. If raised outdoors, cucumbers are ready to be picked in July and August.

Cucumbers are quite versatile, and taste especially good raw in salads. In addition, they can also be worked into warm dishes, canned, or pickled. Fresh cucumbers can be kept for several days in the refrigerator. Keep in mind, though, that if they are kept too cold, they will quickly become soft.

Chilled Cucumber Soup
with Water Biscuits

Peel the cucumbers, chop finely, and lightly salt. Rinse the dill, pat dry, and remove the leaves from the stems. Add the crème fraîche and 3 ounces (100 ml) of water and puree well in a blender. Flavor with salt, pepper, and white balsamic vinegar. Cool completely in the refrigerator.

For the water biscuits, preheat the convection oven to 350° F/180° C (for conventional oven: 390°F/200°C). Combine the flour with 4 teaspoons (20 ml) of water and oil. With a baker's knife, spread the dough thinly onto the baking parchment. Flavor with a little salt and coarsely ground pepper. Bake for 6 minutes until golden brown. Break into pieces and serve with the chilled soup.

FOR THE CHILLED SOUP:
32 oz (900 g) cucumber
1 small bunch of dill
⅓ cup + 1 tablespoon (100 g) crème fraîche
Salt
Pepper
6 tablespoons white balsamic vinegar

FOR THE WATER BISCUITS:
2 teaspoons (10 g) flour
1 teaspoon sunflower oil

ALSO:
Baking parchment

Makes 4 servings
Preparation time: ca. 20 minutes
Chill time: 3 hours
Bake time: 6 minutes

Cucumber Salad
with Shrimp Skewers

10½ oz (300 g) shrimp

2 cucumbers

Salt

2 shallots

1 chili pepper

1 teaspoon small capers

Pepper

4 tablespoons caper water

5 tablespoons olive oil

⅔ cup (150 g) plain yogurt

Cayenne pepper

1 small bunch of dill

ALSO:

8 wooden skewers

Remove the shells from the shrimp and carefully devein with a sharp knife. Rinse in cold water and drain on a paper towel. Clean and seed the cucumbers. Slice the cucumber in thin strips and place in a bowl. Immediately salt, allow to sit for 10 minutes. Then pour off the cucumber water.

Peel and dice the shallots. Clean and dice the chili pepper. Add the shallots, chili pepper, and capers to the cucumber strips. Flavor with pepper. Mix the caper water with 2 tablespoons of olive oil and the yogurt. Season with cayenne pepper and salt. Mix with an immersion mixer until frothy.

Stick the shrimp onto the skewers and season with salt and pepper. Cook the skewers in the remaining olive oil on medium for 2 minutes per side. Plate the cucumber salad and top with ample yogurt sauce. Rinse the dill, blot dry, and pluck the leaves off the stems. Sprinkle the dill over the salad. Place the skewers on the plates and serve.

Makes 4 servings

Preparation time: ca. 30 minutes

Potatoes

Potatoes originally came from South America and were brought to Europe in the sixteenth century. Approximately five thousand different varieties are known around the world, but only a very small number are regularly available in stores. You can differentiate types of potatoes by the time of year in which they are harvested: early, middle, and late potatoes.

Potatoes are enjoyed only when cooked. The peels of fresh, early potatoes contain a significant amount of nutrients and can be eaten. On the other hand, older potatoes have increased quantities of toxins in their skins and should not be consumed. The green spots and eyes should be removed because they can also be poisonous. Potatoes are differentiated by their starch content, so there are appropriate potatoes for most any dish. Waxy potatoes are good for salads and au gratin dishes, and are predominately boiled and used in stews. Floury potatoes are better for soups, purees, or dumplings.

Potato Soup
with Sautéed Arugula

Chop the onions and garlic. Clean the celery and cut into small pieces. Melt the butter in a large pan, and saute' the onions, celery, and garlic for 5 minutes. Peel and roughly chop the potatoes. Add the potatoes to the onion mixture, stirring everything well. Pour in the vegetable broth. Cover and simmer for 30 minutes. Use an immersion mixer to puree the soup, and if desired, strain the soup through a sieve. Add the cream and season with salt, pepper, and nutmeg.

Rinse the arugula. Heat the oil to about 340°F/170°C. Briefly sear the arugula, but stand back from the pan, since the oil may splatter. Drain the arugula on paper towels and add to the soup right before serving.

2 cups (500 g) floury potatoes
2 onions
2 celery stalks
2 tablespoons butter
1 garlic clove
4 cups (1 l) vegetable broth
¾ cup (200 ml) cream
Salt
Pepper
Freshly grated nutmeg

ALSO:
1 bunch of arugula
4 cups (1 l) sunflower oil

Makes 4 servings
Preparation time: ca. 30 minutes
Cook time: ca. 30 minutes

63

Fanned Potatoes with Fresh Garden Herbs

Preheat the convection oven to 340°F/170°C (for conventional oven: 375°F/190°C). Wash the potatoes well and cut into the potatoes, but not all the way through. Cuts should be about 1-inch wide.

Set the potatoes in a baking pan. Wash the herbs and blot dry. Remove the leaves and needles from the stems. Fill the cuts in the potatoes with the herbs. Sprinkle amply with olive oil. Crush the garlic cloves and add to the baking pan. Flavor the potatoes well with Fleur de Sel and pepper. Bake for 50 minutes until crispy.

35 oz (1 kg) medium waxy potatoes
1 bunch of fresh garden herbs (such as sage, thyme, or rosemary)
10 tablespoons olive oil
5 garlic cloves
Fleur de Sel, pepper

Makes 4 servings
Preparation time: ca. 30 minutes
Bake time: 50 minutes

Potato Tart with Pesto

1⅔ cups (200 g) spelt flour

½ cup (100 g) cold butter, cut in
  pieces

½ teaspoon salt

1 egg

35 oz (1 kg) waxy new potatoes

7 tablespoons olive oil

½ cup + 1 tablespoon (150 g)
  crème fraîche

3 oz (80 g) pesto

2 eggs

Pepper

Freshly ground nutmeg

ALSO:

10" tart pan

Butter for the pan

Flour for the work surface

Baking parchment

6 cups (500 g) dried beans
  (for the blind-baking)

For 10" tart pan
Preparation time: ca. 1 hour
Cool time: 30 minutes
Bake time: 30 minutes

Mix the spelt flour, salt, and butter together until crumbs form. Add the egg and quickly knead into a dough. Shape the dough into a ball, wrap in plastic wrap, and set in a cool place for 30 minutes. Peel the potatoes and cut into thin slices. Heat the olive oil and saute' for 10 minutes until they are firm to the bite and golden brown. Occasionally turn the potatoes as they cook. Place potato slices in a bowl.

Preheat the convection oven to 350°F/175°C (for conventional oven: 375°F/190°C). Butter the sides and bottom of the tart pan. Flour the work surface, roll out the dough, and then lay it into the pan. Place the baking parchment on top of the pie crust and weight it down with the dried beans. Bake for 15 minutes. Remove the parchment and the beans.

Stir together the crème fraîche, pesto, and eggs. Season with salt, pepper, and nutmeg. Spread the potato slices on the crust and cover with the egg mixture. Bake for 25 to 30 minutes.

Potato Salad with Broad Beans

Boil the potatoes in salted water. Allow to cool peel, and slice. Chop the bacon and cook until crispy. Remove the bacon from the pan. Dice the shallots and sauté briefly in the bacon grease. Place both the bacon and the shallots in a salad bowl.

Warm up the vegetable broth and mix with mustard. Add the potato slices to the bowl with the bacon and shallots. Cover everything with the broth and white wine vinegar.

Blanch the beans in well-salted water for 3 minutes. Drain and rinse with cold water. Remove the thick hulls by hand and add the beans to salad. Season with the salt and pepper, add the grape seed oil, and carefully combine everything. Rinse the parsley, blot dry, and remove the leaves from the stems. Chop finely and sprinkle on the salad.

5 medium (1 kg) waxy potatoes
Salt
3½ oz (100 g) streaky bacon
2 shallots
¾ cup + 4 teaspoons (200 ml) vegetable broth
1 tablespoon middle-strength mustard
6 tablespoons white wine vinegar
3 cups (300 g) broad beans, shelled
Pepper
2⅛ cups (500 ml) grape seed oil
1 small bunch of parsley

Makes 4 servings
Preparation time: ca. 1½ hours

69

Squash

Originating in America, squash was brought to Europe in the sixteenth century. In order to cultivate squash in your own garden, start raising germlings in pots in late March in order to transplant them to the garden in late May. Be sure to reserve enough room for these plants, since squash is a vine. They grow particularly well on compost piles, which provide the ideal mix of nutrients.

Squash can be prepared various ways in the kitchen. As a side dish, squash is a delicious accompaniment to fish and meat. It can also be canned or worked into soups and breads. When purchasing squash, the stem should be still attached to the fruit. Thump the body of the squash, and if you hear a hollow tone, you can rest assured that your selection is ripe. Squash can be kept for several weeks when stored in a cool, dark location.

Pork Roast with Braised Squash

Preheat the convection oven to 390°F/200°C (for conventional oven: 425°F/220°C). Season the pork roast well with salt and pepper. Place the roast rind down in a roasting pan and pour 2⅛ cups of water into the pan. Braise in the oven for 30 minutes.

Cut the squash in half, remove the seeds, and slice the fruit. Cut the potatoes into quarters. Chop the onion into eighths and slice the garlic. Rinse the thyme, blot dry, and remove the leaves from the stems. Mix all ingredients together in a bowl. Add the salt, pepper, and cayenne pepper and mix well.

Turn the roast over in the pan and cut diamond-hatched slits into the top. Reduce the heat in the convection oven to 350°F/180°C (for conventional oven: 390°F/200°C). Add the vegetables to the pan and braise for another 1½ hours, occasionally pouring beer over the roast. At the end of the cook time, if the skin is not crispy enough, simply place it under the broiler for a few minutes. Remove the roast from the oven and cool for 10 minutes. Slice and place the roast on the plates with the vegetables.

2¼ pounds (1 kg) pork roast
    with rind
Salt
Pepper
1 red kuri squash (800 g)
3 (500 g) small waxy potatoes
2 onions
4 garlic cloves
1 small bunch of thyme
Cyenne pepper
1 bottle of dark beer

ALSO:
Roasting pan

Makes 4 servings
Preparation time: ca. 1 hour
Braise time: 2 hours

Roasted Squash with Burrata

1 red kuri squash (800 g)

3 garlic cloves

5 sprigs of thyme

2 chili peppers

Salt

Pepper

8 tablespoons olive oil

2 bunches of arugula

4 bundles of Burrata cheese

4 tablespoons white balsamic
vinegar

Fleur de Sel

Preheat the convection oven to 350°F/175°C (for conventional oven: 375°F/190°C). Peel the squash, slice in half, and remove the seeds. Cut the fruit into 1-inch thick slices. Crush the garlic. Rinse the thyme, blot dry, and remove the leaves from the stems. Wash the chili peppers cut in half, and remove the seeds. Place everything on a baking sheet and season with salt and pepper. Sprinkle with 5 tablespoons of olive oil and mix everything together with by hand. Braise uncovered in the oven for 15 to 20 minutes

Rinse the arugula and remove the stems. Blot or spin the leaves dry. Divide the braised squash between the plates and top with the arugula and Burrata cheese. Sprinkle with the remaining olive oil and the balsamic vinegar. Season with pepper and Fleur de Sel.

Makes 4 servings

Preparation time: ca. 40 minutes

Bake time: 20 minutes

Squash Quiche

2 cups (275 g) flour
⅓ cup + 1 tbsp (50 g) fresh yeast
½ cup (⅛ l) lukewarm milk
4 eggs
Salt
1 red kuri squash (500 g)
3 tablespoons olive oil
Pepper
Freshly ground nutmeg
Sugar
3 oz (80 g) cubed bacon
1 onion
1 leek stalk
⅔ cup (150 ml) cream
⅓ cup (80 g) Alpine cheese

ALSO:
Flour for the work surface
10" tart pan
Butter and flour for the pan
Baking parchment
Dried beans

For 10" tart pan
Preparation time: ca. 1¼ hours
Rise time: 30 minutes
Bake time: 35 minutes

For the dough, sift flour into a bowl. Dissolve the yeast in the lukewarm milk and add to the flour. Stir in 1 egg, the butter, and ½ teaspoon salt. Knead everything for 5 minutes until a smooth dough forms. Cover the dough and allow to rise in a warm place for 30 minutes.

Preheat the convection oven to 350°F/180°C (for conventional oven: 390°F/200°C). Roll the dough onto a floured work surface. Butter and flour the tart pan. Press the dough into the pan and prick the bottom of the crust with a fork in several places. Place the baking parchment on top of the dough and weight it down with the dried beans. Bake in the oven for 15 minutes.

For the filling, peel, seed, and chop the squash. Sauté in a pan with olive oil for 5 minutes. Season well with salt, pepper, nutmeg, and sugar and remove from the pan. Cook the bacon pieces in the pan. Chop the onion. Clean the leek and cut into rings. Add the onion and leek to the bacon and sauté for another 2 minutes. Distribute the squash and bacon mixture in the quiche crust. Mix the remaining eggs with cream and pour mixture into the quiche crust. Top with the Alpine cheese. Bake for 20 minutes.

Corn

With roots in South America, corn was brought to Europe by Christopher Columbus. To raise corn in your garden, set the seedlings out fairly close together so they can pollinate each other in the bed. In addition, corn requires much sunlight and protection from the wind. The most common variety is sweet corn, although popcorn is also quite popular.

Corn can be prepared all sorts of ways. It is scrumptious in soups, salads, and stews, but it can also be cooked by itself or grilled. Corn tastes best when it has been just picked, since it is at its sweetest point. Fresh corn quickly goes bad, so the cobs should not be stored long.

Corn Fritters

FOR THE FRITTERS:

2 sweet corn cobs

Salt

1¼ cup (150 g) flour

2 tablespoons cream of tartar

⅓ cup (80 ml) milk

2 eggs

½ cup (100 g) fresh herbed
    cheese

1 bunch of dill

Fleur de Sel, pepper

6 tablespoons olive oil

FOR THE DIP:

½ cup + 1 tablespoon (150 g)
    crème fraîche

1 small bunch of parsley

1 chili pepper

Juice from ½ lime

Salt

Pepper

For the fritters, boil the corn in salted water for 15 to 20 minutes until tender. Drain and quickly rinse with cold water. Cut the kernels from the cobs. Combine the flour and cream of tartar in a bowl. In another bowl, mix the milk, eggs, and fresh cheese and stir in the flour mixture. Rinse the dill, blot dry, and chop. Add the dill and corn to the dough. Flavor with Fleur de Sel and pepper.

Heat 2 tablespoons of olive oil and place two tablespoons of the fritter dough in to the pan. Brown for 2 minutes per side. Keep the fritters warm while cooking the remaining dough.

For the dip, place the crème fraîche in a bowl. Rinse the parsley and blot dry. Pluck the leaves from the stems and chop the leaves. Wash and dice the chili pepper. Mix the the creme fraiche, parsley, and chili pepper well. Season with lime juice, salt, and pepper. Serve with the corn fritters.

Tip: Smoked salmon and arugula are especially good paired with the fritters.

Makes 4 servings

Preparation time: ca. 35 minutes

Cook time: 15–20 minutes

Mexican Corn Salad

Boil the corn in a salted water until tender, about 15 to 20 minutes. Drain and rinse in cold water. Cut the kernels from the cobs and fry in 2 tablespoons of olive oil for 5 minutes, stirring constantly. Rinse the kidney beans in running water and mix with the corn in a bowl. Wash the green pepper and the romaine lettuce. Cut into bite-sized pieces and add to the bowl. Rinse the coriander and blot dry, separating the leaves from the stems. Clean the chili peppers. Chop both the coriander and the chili peppers and mix into the rest of the salad.

For the dressing, squeeze the juice from the limes and combine with 3 tablespoons of olive oil, raw cane sugar, Fleur de Sel, and pepper in a screw-top jar. Shake vigorously to combine. Pour the remaining olive oil into a pan. Chop up the tofu and sauté for 5 minutes, stirring constantly. Serve the salad with the roasted tofu and drizzle with the dressing.

3 sweet corn cobs
Salt
7 tablespoons of olive oil
1 can of kidney beans
1 green pepper
1 romaine heart
1 bunch of fresh coriander
2 chili peppers
2 limes
1 teaspoon raw cane sugar
1 teaspoon Fleur de Sel
Dash of fresh pepper
1 package of smoked tofu

Makes 4 servings
Preparation time: ca. 30 minutes
Cook time: 15–20 minutes

Curried Corn Soup
with Coconut Cream

5 sweet corn cobs

Salt

1 onion

2 garlic cloves

2 tablespoons + 2 teaspoons
   (40 g) butter

1 tablespoon curry

⅔ cup (150 ml) white wine

3⅓ cups + 1 tablespoon
   (800 ml) chicken broth

Pepper

ALSO:

¾ cup + 4 teaspoons (200 ml)
   coconut milk (canned)

⅓ cup + 4 teaspoons (100 ml)
   milk

1 tablespoon fish sauce

Boil the corn in salted water until tender for 15 to 20 minutes. Drain and rinse with cold water. Cut the kernels off of the cobs. Dice the onion and garlic. Sauté the onions and garlic in butter. Sprinkle with the curry and sauté a little longer. Add the corn and deglaze with the white wine. Reduce the mixture completely and add the broth at the end. Let the soup simmer for 10 minutes and then puree. Salt and pepper to taste. Strain the soup through a sieve, if desired.

For the coconut cream, mix the coconut milk and milk. Depending on your preference, flavor with either salt or with fish sauce for an Asian flavor. Warm the milk and mix the cream well with either an immersion mixer or a milk frother. Serve the soup in bowls and garnish with the cream.

Makes 4 servings

Preparation time: ca. 40 minutes

Cook time (corn): 15–20 minutes

Cook time (soup): ca. 10 minutes

Chard

Chard, a biennial plant, is native to the Mediterranean and Middle Eastern regions. A member of the beet family, it is available from May through autumn and can be planted between April and June. Although the edible leaves can be harvested during the first year, the flowers and seeds develop in the second year.

Chard is categorized into two groups. Green chard is often prepared much like spinach, and red-ribbed chard has a flavor that resembles asparagus. Chard is also called "the poor man's asparagus." An ideal accompaniment to fish, meat, and egg dishes, it is suitable for steaming, cooking, roasting, and scalloping, as well as for the covering of Rouladen. Wrapped in a damp towel, it can be kept in a refrigerator for one or two days, so it is advisable to use chard immediately.

Veal Cheeks with Chard

2 onions

1 carrot

2 stalks of celery

3 tablespoons sunflower oil

4 veal cheeks

Salt, pepper

1 tablespoon tomato paste

1 tablespoon allspice berries

2 bay leaves

1¼ cup (300 ml) red wine

2 cups (500 ml) beef broth

10½ oz (300 g) chard, washed

Salt

5 tablespoons olive oil

1 small bunch of thyme

Fleur de Sel, pepper, freshly
grated nutmeg

ALSO:

Roasting pan

Makes 4 servings
Preparation time: ca. 1¾ hours
Braise time: 1½ hours

Preheat the convection oven to 350°F/180°C (for conventional oven: 390°F/200°C). Clean and chop the onions, carrot, and celery. Heat the oil in the roasting pan on the stovetop and quickly sear the veal cheeks, seasoning with salt and pepper. Remove the veal and add the vegetables. Cook for 10 minutes, stirring constantly.

Add the tomato paste to the vegetables and simmer briefly. Add back the veal cheeks to the pan and stir in the allspice and bay leaves. Deglaze with red wine and reduce. Pour in the beef broth, cover, and braise in the oven for 1½ hours.

Blanch the chard leaves in salted water for 2 minutes. Rinse in cold water and cut the stems in 4-inch lengths. Sauté in 3 tablespoons of olive oil for 5 minutes. Pluck the thyme leaves from their stems and add to the pan with Fleur de Sel, pepper, and nutmeg. Trim the chard leaves to the same general size and roll them around the stems, securing in place with toothpicks. Sprinkle with olive oil and Fleur de Sel, and serve with polenta.

Remove the veal cheeks from the roasting pan. Simmer the stock for 5 minutes and blend with some of the vegetables. Drain the sauce through a sieve. Slice the meat and serve with the chard and the sauce.

Asian Chard Sandwiches with Honeyed Duck

2 tablespoons sunflower oil

3 duck legs (each 350 g)

Salt

Pepper

3 star anise

2 cups (500 ml) duck broth or
vegetable broth

1 bunch of green onions

2 chili peppers

2 blades of lemon grass

4 tablespoons soy sauce

2 tablespoons honey

Juice of 2 limes

17½ oz (500 g) chard, washed

2 in. ginger

1 tablespoon butter

2 garlic cloves

4 small baguette rolls

ALSO:

Roasting pan

Preheat the convection oven to 350°F/180°C (for conventional oven: 390°F/200°C). Heat the oil in the roasting pan. Season the duck legs with salt and pepper and place in the pan. After 10 minutes, turn the legs and add the star anise. When the legs have gained some color, add the broth. Cover and braise in the oven for 1 hour. Uncover and braise for another 30 to 40 minutes. Cool completely after cooking.

Clean and dice the green onions and chili peppers. Remove the outer leaves and stems of the lemon grass, and finely chop the white part. Debone the duck legs and mix with the green onions, chili peppers and lemon grass. Flavor with the soy sauce, honey, and lime juice. Cut the chard leaves in strips and chop the stems. Peel and dice the ginger. Melt the butter and add the chard stems to the pan. Peel and crush the garlic cloves and add to the pan. Sauté for 8 minutes and add the ginger and the chard leaves. Cook for another 3 minutes, stirring constantly. Season everything with salt and pepper. Remove the garlic cloves from the pan. Cut the baguette rolls and fill with the chard and duck.

Makes 4 servings

Preparation time: ca. 1 hour

Braise time: 1⅔ hours

Carrots

Carrots were first cultivated in the Netherlands during the eighteenth century although their precise origins are still unknown. These root vegetables are planted in May in rows, which are later thinned. They grow best in full sunlight or partial shade.

Carrots can be enjoyed raw, cooked, or braised. Fresh carrots have consistent coloring and are firm and crispy. The carrot rind contains the most nutrients. Since the body has a hard time processing beta carotene found in carrots, cook carrots in a little butter or oil. Store carrots in a cool, dark location, and remove the greenery, since it draws water out of the vegetable. Wash first before preparing them. They can stay good for 2 to 4 weeks.

Braised Carrots
with Star Anise

Peel the carrots and cut in half lengthwise. Caramelize the sugar on high heat until light brown. Add the butter and dissolve the caramel. Deglaze with the white wine, vegetable broth, and orange juice. Add the star anise. Peel and dice the ginger and add to the pan. Flavor with the fish sauce and add the carrots to the broth. Cook the carrots over low heat for about 25 minutes until tender.

Leave the carrots in the broth, cover, and cool overnight to intensify the flavor.

Tip: The anise carrots taste delicious with a grilled pork belly or duck breast.

28 oz (800 g) carrots
¾ cup (150 g) sugar
¼ cup + 2 teaspoons (70 g) butter
¾ cup + 4 teaspoons (200 ml) white wine
1¼ cup (300 ml) vegetable broth
1¼ cup (300 ml) orange juice
6 star anise
1 in. ginger
3 tablespoons fish sauce

Makes 4 servings
Preparation time: ca. 40 minutes
Cook time: ca. 25 minutes

Carrot Salad with Sesame Vinaigrette and Coriander

Peel and grate the carrots and season with salt, pepper, and mirin vinegar.

Peel and dice the ginger. Rinse the coriander, blot dry, and chop finely. Add the ginger and coriander to the carrots and flavor with the sesame oil. Sprinkle with sesame seeds and serve.

Tip: This recipe is a nice way to spice up a simple salad. It also adds a nice touch to a cauliflower salad with curry, chilis, and raisins or a cabbage salad with ginger, honey, and macadamia nuts.

35 oz (1 kg) carrots
Salt, pepper
5 tablespoons mirin vinegar
1½ in. ginger
1 small bunch of coriander
3 tablespoons sesame oil
2 tablespoons sesame seeds

Makes 4 servings
Preparation time: ca. 20 minutes

Peppers

Peppers were brought to Europe in the sixteenth century from Central and South America. Originally, all peppers were spicy, but the mild varieties were cultivated first, which is how the sweet peppers came to be. Paprika plants require much light and warmth. If you raise them in pots, they can be transferred to the garden in May, but they do not survive freezing temperatures.

A pepper's color depends upon its degree of ripeness. Green peppers are immature, but yellow, red, or orange ones are completely ripe. Peppers can be eaten raw or stuffed and used in casseroles or sauces. Since they are sensitive to the cold, store them in a cool location outside of the refrigerator.

Peppers

Pepper Gazpacho with Toasted Ciabatta

1 small onion

1 garlic clove

2 sweet red peppers

12 oz (350 g) cucumber, unpeeled

6 ripe tomatoes

Salt, pepper

5 tablespoons red wine vinegar

6 tablespoons olive oil

ALSO:

1 ciabatta loaf

1 garlic clove

5 tablespoons olive oil

For the gazpacho, dice the onion and garlic. Clean the pepper, remove the stems and seeds, and chop finely. Wash the cucumber and tomatoes, blot dry, and cut into small pieces. Mix everything together and season with salt, pepper, red wine vinegar, and olive oil. Set in the refrigerator to cool completely.

Preheat the convection oven to 375°F/190°C (for conventional oven: 410°F/210°C). Cut the ciabatta into thin slices. Halve the garlic clove and rub onto the slices. Sprinkle with olive oil and toast in the oven for about 10 to 15 minutes. Serve with the gazpacho.

Tip: If you like, add chopped pepper, cucumber, and tomato to the soup.

Makes 4 servings

Preparation time: ca. 30 minutes

Cool time: 3 hours

Bake time: 15 minutes

Merguez with Pepper-Noodle Ragout

Preheat the convection oven to 375°F/190°C (for conventional oven: 410°F/210°C). Wash and quarter the peppers, removing the stems and seeds. Sprinkle salt and pepper onto a baking sheet and lay the peppers on it. Peel the garlic and cut into thin slices. Rinse the thyme, blot dry, and pluck the leaves from the stems.
Top the peppers with the garlic, thyme, along with 4 tablespoons of olive oil. Cover the sheet with aluminum foil and bake for 25 minutes.

Wash the green onions and cut into thin rings. Remove the pan with the peppers from the oven and cool for 15 minutes. Remove the foil and peel and cube the peppers. Pour off the pepper stock from the baking sheet and add the chopped peppers to the stock.

Cook the noodles al dente. Drain the pasta and immediately mix it with the peppers and green onions. Heat the remaining olive oil and brown the merguez on all sides. Divide the pepper noodle ragout between the plates and serve with the sausages.

2 red and 2 yellow sweet
    peppers
2 garlic cloves
Salt
Pepper
1 small bunch of thyme
6 tablespoons olive oil
4 green onions
1¾ cup (350 g) orzo
8 merguez bratwursts

Makes 4 servings
Preparation time: 1 hour
Braise time: 25 minutes

103

Hungarian Goulash

Preheat the convection oven to 350°F/180°C (for conventional oven: 390°F/200°C). Coarsely cube the beef. Peel and chop the onions. Heat the sunflower oil and sear the beef in batches. Do not add too much beef to the pan at one time in order to prevent overcooking. Season with salt and pepper.

Set the beef aside. In the same pan, cook the onion until translucent. Peel and slice the garlic and add to the onions. Return the beef to the pan, and season with both paprika and cumin. Add the tomato paste and marjoram. Stir everything together well. Deglaze with the red wine and reduce by one third. Pour in the beef broth, cover, and braise for 1 hour in the oven.

Wash the peppers, quarter, and remove the stems and seeds. Cut into bite-sized pieces and add to the beef. Braise uncovered for another 40 minutes. Remove from the oven, flavor with salt and pepper, and bring to a boil on the stovetop. Mix the cornstarch with 1 tablespoon of cold water and combine with the goulash. When ready to serve, rinse the marjoram, blot dry, pluck and chop the leaves, and sprinkle on the goulash.

2¼ pound (1 kg) beef
17½ oz (500 g) onions
5 tablespoons sunflower oil
Salt, pepper
3 garlic cloves
1 tablespoon sweet paprika
1 tablespoon spicy paprika
1 teaspoon cumin, minced
1 tablespoon tomato paste
1 tablespoon dried marjoram
1 cup + 2 teaspoons (250 ml)
    red wine
4¼ cups (1 l) beef broth
3 sweet peppers
2 teaspoons corn starch
1 small bunch of fresh
    marjoram

Makes 4 servings
Preparation time: ca. 1 hour
Braise time: 1⅔ hour

Parsnips

Parsnips, which are related to carrots, are planted between March and May and harvested in fall and winter. They are relatively undemanding plants and easy to grow. Frost intensifies the spicy-sweet taste of these root vegetables. In the past, parsnips were widely used but they have faded in popularity with the increased use of potatoes.

Parsnips are often used in purees and can be cooked, roasted, or baked. You can even enjoy them raw. Stored in the refrigerator, these roots can be kept for 1 to 2 weeks.

Parsnip Fries with Curry-Apple Dip

Preheat the convection oven to 350°F/180°C (for conventional oven: 390°F/200°C). Peel the parsnips and slice lengthwise ½-in. thick. Slice again into strips the size of French fries and cut to similar lengths. Spread across a baking dish lined with baking parchment. Sprinkle with the olive oil and season well with Fleur de Sel and pepper. Mix everything together well by hand. Bake for 40 to 50 minutes until crispy. During baking, open the oven two different times to release the steam and allow the parsnips to get even crispier.

For the dip, peel and dice the apple. Combine the crème fraîche with the curry powder and lemon juice. Season with salt and pepper. Stir in the apple cubes. Remove the parsnip fries from the oven and serve immediately with the dip.

FOR THE PARSNIP FRIES:
35 oz (1 kg) parsnips
5 tablespoons olive oil
Fleur de Sel
Pepper

FOR THE DIP:
1 apple
½ cup + 1 tablespoon (150 g) crème fraîche
2 teaspoons curry powder
Juice of ½ lemon
Salt, pepper

ALSO:
Baking parchment

Makes 4 servings
Preparation time: ca. 1 hour
Bake time: 40–50 minutes

Cod with Pureed Parsnips and Browned Butter

Peel and chop the parsnips and potatoes. Just cover with water, and season with salt and lemon juice. Cover, and cook the vegetables until tender. Drain the parsnips and potatoes and allow the moisture in the vegetables to evaporate a little. Add the cream and 2 ounces (50 g) of butter to the vegetables and blend well with an immersion mixer. Flavor with salt, nutmeg, and a splash of lemon juice.

Preheat the convection oven to 350°F/180°C (for conventional oven: 390°F/200°C). Season the cod with salt and pepper. Heat the olive oil and sauté the fish for 2 minutes on each side. End with the skin side down. Flip over and bake for 5 minutes.

Heat the remaining butter until it begins to brown. Then set the pot to a side. Rinse the parsley, blot dry, pluck the leaves from the stems, and chop. Spoon the puree onto the plates and set the cod on top. Sprinkle with the parsley, and pour the browned butter over everything.

28 oz (800 g) parsnips
2 floury potatoes
2 teaspoons salt
Juice from ½ lemon + 1 splash
⅓ cup + 4 teaspoons (100 ml) cream
⅓ pound (150 g) butter
Salt
Freshly ground nutmeg
4 pieces of cod with skin (each 160 g)
Pepper
2 tablespoons olive oil
1 small bunch of parsley

Makes 4 servings
Preparation time: ca. 40 minutes
Bake time: 5 minutes

Radicchio

Radicchio comes from
Italy and has been available
in Northern Europe for
a relatively short time. In
appearance and flavor, it
resembles chicory, but
it is red, which is why it is
sometimes called red chicory.
Depending on the variety,
radicchio is either planted in
the spring and harvested in the
fall, or planted in the summer
and first cut in the spring.
Frost intensifies the color of its
characteristically red leaves.

Radicchio has a strong, slightly
bitter flavor. It lends salads
a bright note, and when
blanched or steamed, it goes
well with meat or fish. If stored
in a cool location, it can be
kept for 5 to 7 days.

Red Wine Risotto with Roasted Radicchio

For the risotto, peel and dice the shallots and lightly crush the clove. Add the garlic and shallots to a pan with olive oil. Cook over medium heat until translucent. Add the risotto rice and stir. Deglaze with red wine and reduce. Add more wine and reduce again. Stir constantly so the risotto does not stick. Repeat this process until all of the red wine has been used. Do the same with the broth. After about 25 minutes, the rice should be a little firm and have a creamy consistency.

Clean and halve the radicchio. Wrap 2 slices of bacon around each part. In a large pan, heat the olive oil and sauté the radicchio for about 3 to 4 minutes. Then add the powdered sugar and caramelize. Deglaze with balsamic vinegar and reduce almost completely. Pour the chicken broth into the pan and boil briefly.

Flavor the risotto with parmesan cheese, butter, and sugar. Season with salt and pepper and stir. Divide the risotto between the plates and place 2 radicchio halves on each portion. Sprinkle with pan drippings.

FOR THE RISOTTO:

1 shallot

1 garlic clove

3 tablespoons olive oil

12 oz (350 g) risotto rice

2⅛ cup (500 ml) red wine

1¾ cups (400 ml) chicken broth

2 oz (60 g) grated parmesan

3 oz (80 g) butter

1 tablespoon sugar

Salt

Pepper

FOR THE RADICCHIO:

4 radicchio trevisano

16 strips lean bacon

3 tablespoons olive oil

2 tablespoons powdered sugar

4 tablespoons balsamic vinegar

⅓ cup + 4 teaspoons (100 ml) chicken broth

Makes 4 servings
Preparation time: ca. 40 minutes
Cook time: ca. 25 minutes

Warm Orange Radicchio with Veal Steaks

3 oranges

4 radicchio trevisano

4 tablespoons olive oil

1 tablespoon powdered sugar

Salt, pepper

1 tablespoon butter

2 tablespoons white balsamic
  vinegar

4 veal steaks (each 150 g)

1 tablespoon fennel seeds

Filet the oranges and place in a bowl. Squeeze the rest of the pulp and catch the juice in a container. Wash the radicchio, cut in half, and remove the stem. Cut the leaves into bite-sized pieces.

Heat 1 tablespoon of olive oil and immediately add the powdered sugar to caramelize. Add the radicchio and sauté for 3 minutes, stirring constantly. Season with salt and pepper. Add the butter and let froth. Deglaze with the orange juice and flavor with the balsamic vinegar. Add the radicchio to the orange slices in the bowl and marinate.

Season the veal steaks with salt and pepper. Grind the fennel seeds in a mortar or chop coarsely with a knife. Sprinkle on the steaks. Heat the remaining olive oil in the pan and sauté the veal steaks for about 1 minute per side. Immediately wrap in aluminum foil and marinate for 5 minutes. Serve the steaks with the salad.

Makes 4 servings

Preparation time: ca. 40 minutes

Red Beets

Red Beets are a type of turnip that has been cultivated in Germany for centuries and are easy to raise. Before planting, the seeds should be soaked in water. The sowing time for beets is from late April to July, and starting in August, they can be harvested. Beets should not be allowed to grow too large since they get woodier on the inside the bigger they get. Keep this in mind when buying beets as well.

Red beets can be enjoyed raw. When working with beets, try not to get any juice on you because red color, which is used as a basis for food coloring, is very hard to remove. If stored in a cool, dry location, beets will keep for a long time.

Braised Red Beets
with Cumin

35 oz (1 kg) red beets
3 shallots
3 garlic cloves
5 tablespoons olive oil
2 tablespoons Fleur de Sel
1 tablespoon sugar
2 teaspoons cumin seeds
⅔ cup (150 ml) orange juice
¾ cup + 4 teaspoons (200 ml)
    chicken broth
5 tablespoons red wine vinegar

ALSO:
roasting pan
baking parchment

Preheat the convection oven to 350°F/180°C (for conventional oven: 390°F/200°C). Peel and slice the beets. Peel and halve the shallots. Crush the garlic cloves lightly and combine all ingredients in a roasting pan. Sprinkle with olive oil and season with Fleur de Sel and sugar. Chop the cumin seeds and add the cumin, orange juice, chicken broth, and red wine vinegar to the pan.

Cover with baking parchment and braise in the oven for 2 hours. Remove the baking parchment in the last half hour.

Tip: Serve warm with sour cream and toasted bread.

Makes 4 servings
Preparation time: ca. 20 minutes
Braise time: 2 hours

Red Beet Salad

For the salad, add the beets, salt, cumin, and red wine vinegar to a pot. Add enough water to cover the vegetables. Cook for 60 to 90 minutes until tender. Drain the beets and allow to cool. Slice the beets thinly and place in a bowl.

For the dressing, peel and halve the onions. Add the onion, red wine vinegar, grape seed oil, sugar, salt, and pepper to the beets. Rinse the chives, blot dry, and chop. Sprinkle on top of the salad.

Tip: Prepare the salad the day before serving and marinate overnight. It tastes the best at this point.

FOR THE SALAD:

2¼ lb. red beets

1 teaspoon salt

1 teaspoon cumin

5 tablespoons red wine vinegar

FOR THE DRESSING:

1 onion

4 tablespoons red wine vinegar

4 tablespoons grape seed oil

2 teaspoons sugar

Salt, pepper

1 bunch of chives

Makes 4 servings
Preparation time: ca. 40 minutes
Cook time: 60–90 minutes

Red Beet Tarte Flambée

FOR THE TOPPING:
17½ oz (500 g) red beets
1 teaspoon salt
1 teaspoon cumin
5 tablespoons red wine vinegar
¾ cup + 1 tablespoon (200 g) crème fraîche
4 green onions
4 tablespoons olive oil
Fleur de Sel
Pepper
3 oz (80 g) parmesan cheese

FOR THE DOUGH:
1⅔ cup (200 g) flour
2 tablespoons sunflower oil
½ teaspoon salt

ALSO:
Flour for the work surface

For the topping, combine the beets, salt, cumin, and red wine vinegar in a pot. Fill with enough water to cover the vegetables completely. Cover and simmer for 60 to 90 minutes until tender. Cool slightly, peel, and slice thinly.

For the dough, combine the flour, oil, ½ cup + 1 teaspoon (125 ml) water, and salt. Knead until smooth. Cover with plastic wrap and let rise for 20 minutes. Preheat the convection oven to 375°F/190°C (for conventional oven: 410°F/210°C). Flour the work surface and turn the dough out onto it. Roll the dough to a thickness of ⅛ inch and place onto the baking sheet lined with baking parchment.

Spread the crème fraîche onto the dough. Clean the green onions, cut into rings, and sprinkle onto the dough along with the beets. Drizzle olive oil onto the tart and season with Fleur de Sel and pepper. Bake for 25 minutes. Grate parmesan cheese onto the tart.

Makes 4 servings
Preparation time: ca. 1 hour
Cook time: 60–90 minutes
Bake time: 25 minutes

Red Beets with Horseradish Crème and Smoked Trout

Combine the beets, salt, cumin, and 4 tablespoons of red wine vinegar in a pot. Add enough water to cover the vegetables completely. Simmer covered for 60 to 90 minutes until tender. Let the beets cool slightly and peel. Chop the beets and mix into a smooth cream with ⅓ cup + 4 teaspoons (100 g) of butter, the creamed horseradish, and the remaining red wine vinegar. Cool for 1 hour. Rinse the chives and blot dry. Chop and stir into the cream.

Remove the seeds from the apples and cut into 1½ inch thick slices. Caramelize the sugar and add the apples and the remaining butter. Cook the apples for 2 to 3 minutes, turning frequently.

Spread the beet crème onto the pumpernickel slices and top with the warm apples. Cut the smoked trout into pieces and place on top. Flavor with freshly ground pepper.

14 oz (400 g) red beets
1 teaspoon salt
1 teaspoon cumin
6 tablespoons red wine vinegar
½ cup + 2 teaspoons (130 g) butter
3 tablespoons creamed horseradish
1 bunch of chives
2 apples
2 tablespoons sugar
8 slices of pumpernickel bread
7 oz (200 g) smoked trout
Pepper

Makes 4 servings
Preparation time: ca. 30 minutes
Cook time: 60–90 minutes

127

Asparagus

Asparagus is the king of the vegetable world. However, its cultivation requires much patience, and it takes three years before the first white, green, or purple stems can be picked. The harvest period falls between mid-April and the Feast of St. John the Baptist on June 24.

Asparagus must be prepared quickly. The fresher it is, the better it tastes. You can recognize fresh asparagus by its firmly closed heads and the squeakiness when you rub the stems against each other. Always peel asparagus from top to bottom, leave the tips untouched, and cut off the woody stem bottoms. When cooking, be sure to use a sufficiently large pot. Wrapped in a damp towel, asparagus will stay good for several days in the refrigerator.

Asparagus with
Radish-Chive Vinaigrette

FOR THE ASPARAGUS:

70½ oz (2 kg) white asparagus

4 tablespoons canola oil

Salt

Sugar

⅔ cup (160 ml) dry white wine

FOR THE VINAIGRETTE:

2 bunches of radishes

5 tablespoons canola oil

4 tablespoons apple cider vinegar

Salt

Pepper

2 tablespoons honey

1 bunch of chives

ALSO:

Baking parchment

Preheat the convection oven to 350°F/180°C (for conventional oven: 390°F/200°C). Peel the asparagus and cut off the woody ends. Divide into 4 portions and place each on its own piece of baking parchment. Drizzle 1 tablespoon of canola oil over each portion and season with salt and sugar. Fold the ends of the baking parchment, pour ⅛ cup + 2 teaspoons (40 ml) of white wine on each portion, and close into compact packets. Set the packets on a baking pan and braise in the oven for 30 minutes.

For the vinaigrette, wash the radishes, slice, and cut into narrow strips. Mix the canola oil, cider vinegar, salt, pepper, and honey in a bowl. Add the radishes and stir well. Remove the asparagus from the oven, open the packets, and spoon the marinated radishes on each portion. Rinse the chives and blot dry. Chop and sprinkle them onto the asparagus.

Makes 4 servings

Preparation time: ca. 50 minutes

Braise time: 30 minutes

Asparagus Quiche with Gruyère

For the dough, combine the quark, milk, oil, and salt. Mix the flour with the cream of tartar and add to the quark mixture. Knead everything into a smooth dough, wrap in plastic wrap, and let rise until ready to bake.

For the filling, peel and chop the potatoes. Boil for 15 minutes in salted water until tender. Preheat the convection oven to 375°F/190°C (for conventional oven: 390°F/200°C). Butter and flour the baking dish. Roll out the dough to a thickness of ¼ inch and place in the dish. Cut away any dough that laps over the dish edges.

Drain the cooked potatoes and mash them with the Gruyère. Add the eggs and sour cream. Mix with salt, pepper, and a pinch of nutmeg. Rinse the asparagus, cut off the woody ends, and place on top of the dough. Spread the potato-cheese mixture on top of the asparagus. Bake the quiche for about 30 minutes in the oven until golden brown. Cool for at least 10 minutes.

FOR THE DOUGH:
5 oz (150 g) low-fat quark
6 tablespoons milk
6 tablespoons sunflower oil
1 teaspoon salt
2⅔ cups (300 g) flour
1 packet cream of tartar

FOR THE FILLING:
17 ½ oz (500 g) potatoes
Salt
1¾ cup (200 g) Gruyère cheese, finely grated
3 eggs
1¾ cup (400 g) sour cream
Pepper
Freshly grated nutmeg
2 bunches of green asparagus

ALSO:
1 rectangular baking dish
Butter and flour for the dish

For 1 rectangular baking dish
Preparation time: ca. 1½ hours
Cook time: ca. 15 minutes
Bake time: 30 minutes

Asparagus with Ramson Hollandaise Sauce

70½ oz (2 kg) white asparagus

1 cup + two teaspoons (250 g) butter

Salt

2 tablespoons sugar

Juice of 1 lemon + 1 splash

1 shallot

1 bay leaf

4 peppercorns

4 tablespoons white balsamic vinegar

3 egg yolks

1 bunch of ransom

1 pinch cayenne

ALSO:

16 slices Wacholder ham

Peel the asparagus and cut off the woody ends. Simmer the asparagus peels in water for about 10 minutes. Remove and add ¼ cup (50 g) of butter, 2 teaspoons salt, sugar, and lemon juice to the water. Put the peeled asparagus back into the simmering water, and cook for about twelve minutes.

Melt the remaining butter. Peel the shallots, coarsely chop, and place into another small pot with the bay leaf, peppercorns, balsamic vinegar, and ⅓ cup + 4 teaspoons (100 ml) of water. Bring to a boil, and reduce by one third. Cool slightly and pour through a sieve. Combine the egg yolks with the reduction in a metal bowl and set over a pot of simmering water. Stir the mixture with a whisk until a thick, yet fluid, cream forms. Remove from the stovetop and pour the warm butter as a thin stream into the mixture, stirring constantly.

Clean the ransom, blot dry, and slice into strips. Mix into the hollandaise sauce. Season with some salt, cayenne, and a splash of lemon juice. Remove the asparagus from the stock and place on the plates. Serve with the hollandaise sauce and the Wacholder ham.

Makes 4 servings

Preparation time: ca. 1 hour

Cook time (stock): ca. 10 minutes

Cook time (asparagus): ca. 12 minutes

Spinach

Beginning in March, spinach can be planted directly into the bed and is ready to be picked in a relatively short time. If you cut the leaves free at the base of the roots, the spinach will grow back and can be harvested again. For the fall harvest, spinach must be planted in August. The winter-hardy varieties can be picked in spring.

Young raw spring spinach tastes best in a salad. However, if blanched, it is good in pasta or as a side dish or filling. Spinach contains nitrate, which can be transformed into toxic substances, so it is best to prepare spinach when still fresh and eat it immediately. Blanching reduces the amount of nitrate, but the cooking water should not be used for anything else. Spinach can stay fresh in the refrigerator for up to 2 days.

Spinach-Ricotta Pockets

Wash the spinach and spin dry. Remove the hard stems and set a side. Peel and dice the shallot and garlic. Sauté in a pan with the butter until translucent. Add the spinach and cook briefly until the leaves wilt. Season with salt, pepper, and nutmeg. Remove from the pan, cool, and squeeze lightly by hand.

Combine the ricotta with the parmesan cheese in a bowl. Add the spinach and mix well. Preheat the convection oven to 350°F/180°C (for conventional oven: 390°F/200°C). Melt the butter in a small pot. Spread out the strudel dough sheets and brush amply with butter. Sprinkle with bread crumbs and add 2 tablespoons of spinach-ricotta filling to each sheet. Carefully roll up the sheets and press the ends together. Brush once again with butter and bake for 20 minutes until golden brown. Serve warm.

17½ oz (500 g) fresh spinach
1 shallot
1 garlic clove
1 tablespoon butter
Salt, pepper, freshly grated
    nutmeg
⅔ cup (150 g) ricotta
¾ cup (80 g) parmesan cheese,
    grated
8 strudel dough sheets

ALSO:
⅓ cup (80 g) butter for brushing
4 tablespoons bread crumbs

Makes 8 pockets
Preparation time: ca. 1 hour
Bake time: 20 minutes

Spinach Strudel with Salmon

2 shallots

1 garlic clove

2 tablespoons butter

21 oz (600 g) fresh spinach, washed

Salt, pepper, freshly grated nutmeg

17½ oz (500 g) puff pastry, thawed

4 tablespoons bread crumbs

25 oz (700 g) salmon

4 tablespoons sweet chili sauce

1 egg yolk

2 tablespoons cream

ALSO:

Flour for the work surface

Makes 4 servings

Preparation time: ca. 1 hour

Bake time: 30 minutes

Peel and chop the shallots and garlic. Froth the butter in a pan and add the shallots and garlic. Sauté briefly. Immediately add the spinach and cook until it wilts. Season with some salt, pepper, and nutmeg. Pour the mixture into a sieve and let drain.

Preheat the convection oven to 390°F/200°C (for conventional oven: 425°F/220°C). Place the puff pastry pieces onto the floured work surface, overlapping the edges a little to make a 12" x 16" rectangle. Sprinkle with some flour, and roll the dough out a little thinner. Spread the bread crumbs across the dough. Squeeze the liquid from the spinach by hand and spoon across the right side of the dough. Trim the fish into a rectangular filet. Season with salt and pepper and coat with the sweet chili sauce. Place the fish on top of the spinach. Fold the dough over so that it creates a closed pocket. Press the two short edges down and press firmly with a fork.

Line a baking sheet with baking parchment. Stir the egg yolk into the cream and brush onto the strudel. Score the top of the pastry with diamond shapes. Bake for 15 minutes. Reduce the heat to 350°F and bake for another 15 minutes. Remove from the oven and slice to serve.

Tomatoes

Tomatoes originally come from South America and belong to the nightshade family of plants. This popular vegetable is available in a wide array of colors. The seedlings should first be planted in the bed after May, since tomatoes cannot tolerate frost. They thrive in direct sun and need to be fertilized and watered regularly. However, the sensitive leaves should not come in contact with water.

Whether as a salad or soup, in sauces or chutneys, as a filling, or grilled, tomatoes work wonderfully in a broad number of dishes. The green parts of the plant and the immature fruits are poisonous and should not be consumed. Tomatoes keep best when stored at room temperature.

Mixed Tomatoes
with Crispies

Preheat the convection oven to 390°F/200°C (for
conventional oven: 425°F/220°C). Spread the phyllo
dough sheets on the work surface. Melt the butter, and
brush onto the dough. Cut each sheet into 3 strips. Fold
each 3 times and place on a baking sheet lined with
baking parchment. Bake for about 8 minutes until golden
brown. Cool.

Wash the tomatoes and remove the cores. Slice both
the tomatoes and the buffalo mozzarella. Stack the
ingredients, alternating the cheese and the tomatoes with
the crispy phyllo dough, and season with Fleur de Sel and
pepper. Drizzle with the olive oil. Rinse the basil, blot
dry, and pluck the leaves from the stems. Sprinkle on the
tomatoes and serve immediately.

4 phyllo dough sheets
¼ cup + 2 teaspoons (70 g)
    butter
4 large green tomatoes
2 rounds of buffalo mozzarella
Fleur de Sel, pepper
8 tablespoons premium olive oil
1 bunch of basil

ALSO:
Baking parchment

Makes 4 servings
Preparation time: ca. 30 minutes
Bake time: 8 minutes

Bright Tomato Pizza with Pesto

FOR THE DOUGH:

2½ cups (300 g) flour

4 teaspoons (20 g) fresh yeast

½ cup + 2 tablespoons (150 ml)
   lukewarm water

3 tablespoons olive oil

½ teaspoon salt

FOR THE TOPPING:

4 large bright tomatoes, such as
   bull's heart tomatoes

5 tablespoons pesto sauce

2 large mozzarella rounds

Coarsely ground pepper

1 bunch of fresh basil

ALSO:

Flour for the work surface

For the dough, put the flour in a bowl, and form a hollow in the middle. Crumble the yeast and stir into the flour along with 3 tablespoons + 1 teaspoon (50 ml) of water. Cover with plastic wrap and let rise at room temperature for 15 minutes.

Preheat the convection oven to 390°F/200°C (for conventional oven: 425°F/220°C). Add the olive oil, salt, and the remaining water. Knead all of the ingredients into a smooth dough. Cover and let rise for another 45 minutes /until the dough doubles in size. Divide the dough into 5 portions and form each into a ball. Allow the balls to relax and then roll the balls out thinly on the floured work surface.

For the topping, wash and slice the tomatoes. Lay them on the pizzas and bake them for 15 minutes on a baking sheet lined with baking parchment. Remove from the oven and spread the pesto and the sliced mozzarella on top of the tomatoes. Bake for another 5 minutes. Season with pepper. Rinse the basil, blot dry, and before serving, scatter the basil over the pizzas.

Makes 5 pizzas

Preparation time: ca. 45 minutes

Rise time: 1 hour

Bake time: 20 minutes

Nice-Style Baguette with Aioli

17½ (500 g) cocktail tomatoes
4 tablespoons olive oil
Fleur de Sel
Pepper
5 thyme stems

2 egg yolks
1 heaping teaspoon mustard
½ cup + 2 tablespoons (150 ml)
 olive oil
2 garlic cloves
Salt
3 tablespoons lemon juice

½ cup (100 g) beans
8 quail eggs
2 small romaine hearts
2 cans tuna fish
10 caper berries

ALSO:
1 baguette, halved lengthways
Baking parchment

Makes 2 baguette halves
Preparation time: ca. 1 hour
Dry time: 5 hours

Preheat the convection oven to 140°F/60°C (for conventional oven: 175°F/80°C). Wash the cocktail tomatoes, cut in half, and place on a pan lined with baking parchment. Drizzle with olive oil and season with Fleur de Sel and pepper. Rinse the thyme, blot dry, remove the leaves from the stems, and sprinkle over the tomatoes. Leave the pan in the oven for 5 hours. Crack the oven door during baking, so the tomatoes can dry better.

For the aioli, blend the egg yolks and mustard with a mixer. Add the olive oil in a thin stream, beating continuously. Peel and dice the garlic cloves. Add the garlic, salt, pepper, and lemon juice to the mayonnaise. Mix well.

Blanch the beans for about 8 minutes in salted water. Drain and rinse in cold water, and cut into thin slices. Cook the quail eggs for 3 minutes. Remove rinse in cold water, and peel. Rinse the romaine lettuce and tear into bite-sized pieces. Drain the tuna. Spread a generous amount of aioli onto the baguette and top with the lettuce and tuna. Place the dried tomatoes on top. Next spread the beans across the tomatoes. Halve the quail eggs and add them and the caper berries. Season with Fleur de Sel and pepper.

Three-Part Bruschetta

Preheat the convection oven to 350°F/180°C (for conventional oven: 390°F/200°C). Cut the baguette diagonally, making slices ¾ in. thick. Sprinkle with 2 tablespoons of olive oil. Peel and halve the garlic cloves, placing them on the baguette slices. Roast the baguettes in the oven for 10 to 15 minutes until golden brown.

Wash and quarter the tomatoes. Remove the stems and seeds and cube. Put each variety into its own bowl and season heartily with salt, pepper, and sugar. Let the tomatoes sit for 30 minutes and then drain off the water. Wash the basil, pluck the leaves from the stems, and chop coarsely. Mix the basil and the remaining olive oil into the tomatoes. Spread the tomatoes amply onto the toasted baguette slices and serve immediately.

1 small baguette
8 tablespoons premium olive oil
1 garlic clove
4 yellow, 4 black, and 4 red tomatoes
Salt
Pepper
Sugar
1 bunch of basil

Makes 4 servings
Preparation time: ca. 40 minutes
Bake time: 10–15 minutes

Seafood Salad with Tomato Vinaigrette

Clean the musky octopuses, rinse under cold water, and combine in a pot with 4¼ cups (1 l) of water, the white wine, bay leaves, peppercorns, 2 garlic cloves, and thyme. Season well with salt and simmer for about 1 hour.

Remove the stems of the tomatoes and score the bottoms lightly with an X. Blanch the tomatoes in boiling water for 15 to 20 seconds, immediately rinsing in cold water. Skin, seed, and chop the tomatoes, and place in a large bowl. Rinse the chives and blot dry, cut them into little rolls. Add the chives, 6 tablespoons of olive oil, lemon juice, and ⅓ cup + 4 teaspoons (100 ml) of cooking stock to the tomatoes. Remove the octopuses from the stock and cut into small pieces. Add the octopuses to the bowl and mix everything well.

Thinly slice the baguette and toast in a hot pan with the remaining olive oil and one crushed garlic clove. Place the marinated musky octopuses, tomato vinaigrette, and the baguette slices on soup plates. Sprinkle with pepper and serve.

Tip: If you do not care for musky octopus, fried calamari can be used instead in this salad.

FOR THE SALAD:
20 musky octopuses
2⅛ cups (½ l) white wine
2 bay leaves
10 peppercorns
3 garlic cloves
1 small bunch of thyme
Salt

FOR THE VINAIGRETTE:
4 tomatoes
1 small bunch of chives
8 tablespoons olive oil
Juice of 1 lemon
Coarsely ground pepper

ALSO:
1 small baguette

Makes 4 portions
Preparation time: ca. 1⅓ hours
Cook Time: 1 hour

White Cabbage

White cabbage originally came from the Mediterranean region. Even though it is a fall and winter vegetable, there are some varieties that ripen in June. The cultivation of cabbage is uncomplicated. However, the plants require significant room to grow, and they are not ready to pick until 6 months after planting.

The most well-known form of white cabbage is sauerkraut, but the vegetable is great in cabbage roulade and stews. Before cooking, chop the cabbage as small as possible. This will reduce the cook time and help retain the leaves' nutrients. The addition of cumin makes cabbage easier to digest. If stored in a cool, dry location, white cabbage can keep for a long time. After it has been cut into, it should be stored in the refrigerator.

Coleslaw with T-Bone Steaks

For the coleslaw, remove the outer leaves of the white cabbage. Cut the head in half, and remove the stem. Quarter each half, and rinse under cold water. With a plane or a sharp knife, slice the white cabbage into thin strips. Peel the carrots and onions and cut into thin strips.

Preheat the convection oven to 350°F/180°C (for conventional oven: 390°F/200°C). Put the cabbage and onion strips into a bowl and salt well. Knead the mixture for several minutes with your fingers and then add the carrots. Combine the mayonnaise and sour cream. Season with lemon juice, pepper, and cayenne. Add this mixture to the cabbage, and mix everything well.

For the steaks, season the meat with salt and pepper. Heat the sunflower oil and sear the steaks on both sides for 2 minutes per side. Crush the garlic cloves and add to the pan. Place the steaks into a baking dish. Cook in the oven for 12 to 15 minutes. Froth the butter in a pan and add the rosemary. At the end of the cook time, pour the butter onto the steaks. Let the steaks rest for 5 minutes. Cut the meat from the bones and slice. Season with Fleur de Sel and pepper and serve with the coleslaw.

FOR THE COLESLAW:

1 head of white cabbage

3 carrots

1 onion

Salt

3½ tablespoons (50 g) mayonnaise

½ cup (100 g) sour cream

Juice of 1 lemon

Pepper

Cayenne Pepper

FOR THE STEAKS:

2 T-bone steaks (17½ oz [500 g] each)

Salt

Pepper

5 tablespoons sunflower oil

2 garlic cloves

2 tablespoons + teaspoon (50 g) butter

1 rosemary branch

Fleur de Sel

Makes 4 servings
Preparation time: ca. 1 hour
Cook time: 12–15 minutes

Asian Cabbage Wraps

1 head of white cabbage
Salt
1 day-old roll
22 oz (600 g) mixed ground
 meat
2 eggs
7½ tablespoons (40 g) ginger
2 garlic cloves
1 bunch green onions
1 red and 1 green chili pepper
Pepper
3 tablespoons sunflower oil
¾ cup + 4 teaspoons (200 ml)
 chicken broth
6 tablespoons sweet chili sauce

ALSO:
Cooking twine
Roasting pan

Makes 8-10 cabbage wraps
Preparation time: ca. 1½ hours
Cook time: 10 minutes
Braise time: 40 minutes

Remove the outer leaves of the white cabbage and cut away the stem. Blanch the head for 10 minutes in salted water. Rinse in cold water. Separate the leaves from each other and let drip dry. Separate 8 to 10 large leaves and set the rest of the leaves aside.

Preheat the convection oven to 340°F/170°C (for conventional oven: 375°F/190°C). Soak the roll in water for 5 minutes. Squeeze out the water and place in a bowl. Add the ground meat and eggs to the bowl. Peel and dice the ginger and garlic. Rinse the green onions and cut into thin rings. Wash, halve, seed, and dice the red and green chili peppers. Add everything to the meat, season with salt and pepper, and stir.

Spoon 2 to 3 tablespoons of the meat mixture onto each of the large cabbage leaves. Fold the sides up and roll tightly. With a piece of cooking twine, tie each into a wrap. Place the cabbage wraps into a pan with sunflower oil and sear on all sides until the wraps gain some color. Slice the remaining leaves into thin strips and sauté in the pan as well. Place both the cabbage wraps and strips into the roasting pan. Pour the chicken broth into the pan and mix with the sweet chili sauce. Braise for 40 minutes.

Zucchini

Zucchini is a vine and is a relative of squash. Zucchini are easy to raise, but, they require much water, regular fertilization, and ample space, especially if you do not trim them back occasionally. They can be planted in late May and harvested between June and October. Zucchini tastes the best when small and young. After each picking, the plants produce more blooms, so you can harvest zucchini several times.

Zucchini are especially good in Mediterranean dishes. They can be eaten raw, fried, baked, or sautéed. Even the blossoms can be consumed. If kept in the refrigerator, zucchini remain good for 1 or 2 weeks.

Zucchini Rolls with Goat Cheese

2 small yellow and 2 small
    green zucchini
10 tablespoons olive oil
1 rosemary branch
Salt
Pepper
1 cup (300 g) fresh goat cheese
⅓ cup + 1 tablespoon (100 g)
    crème fraîche
3 tomatoes
1 shallot
3 tablespoons sherry vinegar
2 tablespoons honey

Clean the zucchini and cut into very thin strips lengthwise with a food slicer. Heat a grill pan and sear the zucchini strips with 5 tablespoons of olive oil for 1 minute per side. Rinse the rosemary branch, blot dry, and pluck off the needles. Add the needles to the zucchini. Remove the pan from the stovetop and let the zucchini strips sit for a few minutes. Season with salt and pepper.

In a bowl, combine the fresh goat cheese with the crème fraîche and spoon the mixture into an icing bag. Overlap two zucchini strips and do this with the rest of the strips. Squirt the goat cheese onto the strips and carefully roll them up.

Remove the stems of the tomatoes and lightly score an X onto the bottoms. Blanch for 15 to 20 seconds and immediately rinse in cold water. Skin, seed, and chop the tomatoes, placing them in a small bowl. Peel and dice the shallot, and add it to the tomatoes along with the sherry vinegar, remaining olive oil, and honey. Season with salt and pepper. Place the goat cheese rolls onto a plate and drizzle with the tomato vinaigrette.

Makes 16–20 rolls
Preparation time: ca. 1 hour

Stuffed Zucchini Blossoms

1 small zucchini
2 tablespoons olive oil
Salt
Pepper
⅓ cup (60 g) pine nuts
1 cup (250 g) ricotta cheese
2 eggs
1 garlic clove
3 oz (80 g) parmesan cheese
½ teaspoon chili flakes
8 zucchini blossoms + 1 small
   zucchini

1 egg white
¼ teaspoon baking powder
½ cup (60 g) flour
⅓ cup + 2 tablespoons (50 g)
   corn starch
1 teaspoon salt
½ cup + 2 tablespoons (150 ml)
   ice cold water

ALSO:
4¼ cups (1 l) sunflower oil for
   frying

Clean and dice the zucchini. Sear for 2 minutes in olive oil. Season with salt and pepper. Place the zucchini in a bowl. Roast the pine nuts, chop coarsely, and add to the zucchini cubes. Add the ricotta cheese. Beat the eggs and dice the garlic, stirring both into the ricotta mixture. Grate the parmesan cheese and add it and the chili flakes to the ricotta mixture.

Carefully open the zucchini blossoms. Remove the flower stems and briefly rinse out the flowers. Fill them with the ricotta mixture using an icing bag. Carefully press the flowers closed around the filling.

Heat the sunflower oil to 350°F/180°C. Combine the baking powder, flour, corn starch, and salt. Lightly beat the egg white and add water. Pour into the flour mixture and stir everything together. Carefully coat the zucchini blossoms with the dough and fry only two together at a time until the crust is golden brown. Drain on paper towels.

Tip: Instead of frying, you can also steam the zucchini blossoms for 12 to 15 minutes over low heat.

Makes 8 stuffed zucchini blossoms
Preparation time: ca. 45 minutes

Onions

Used in Ancient Egypt, onions have been valued for many centuries as flavoring agents and medicinal plants. Usually onions are planted in March, and harvested in early fall. Winter varieties are set out in August. If you plant bulbs, they will be ready to pick during the summer. Onions prefer sunny locations and do not grow well if the conditions are too damp.

There is a suitable onion for every dish. The various types differ from each other according to their sharpness and sweetness. Countless dishes, such as soups, sauces, salads, and breads, are totally unthinkable without this popular vegetable. Onions should be stored in dark, cool, and dry locations, best in the cellar or cupboard. Depending on the type, they can stay good from several weeks to several months.

Pearl Onion Focaccia

FOR THE FOCACCIA:

4¼ cup (500 g) flour

1½ tablespoons (20 g) fresh yeast

1 cup + 2 teaspoons (250 ml) lukewarm water

6 tablespoons olive oil

1 teaspoon salt

FOR THE TOPPING:

17½ oz (500 g) pearl onions

1 tablespoon butter

¾ cup + 4 teaspoons (200 ml) port

2 tablespoons sugar

Salt

Pepper

1 bay leaf

8 tablespoons balsamic vinegar

ALSO:

1 8" springform pan

Oil for brushing

Makes 1 8" springform pan

Preparation time: ca. 1½ hours

Rise time: ca. 55 minutes

Bake time: 30 minutes

For the focaccia, pour the flour into a bowl and make a trough in the center. Dissolve the yeast in ⅓ cup + 4 teaspoons (100 ml) of water and pour into the trough. With some flour from the edges, make a yeast sponge. Cover and let rise for 15 minutes in a warm place. Afterward, add the remaining water, 4 tablespoons of olive oil, and salt. Knead for several minutes into a smooth dough and return to the bowl. Let rise for another 40 minutes, doubling in size.

Preheat the convection oven to 350°F/180°C (for conventional oven: 390°F/200°C). For the topping, peel the pearl onions. Melt the butter and add the onions. Sauté for 5 minutes. Deglaze with the port and season with sugar, salt, and pepper. Add the bay leaf and balsamic vinegar. Simmer for 10 minutes and reduce.

Brush the edges of the springform pan with oil. Spoon the onions into the pan and add several tablespoons of stock. Place the risen dough into the pan and press down lightly. Brush with the remaining olive oil. Bake for 30 minutes. Remove from the pan and let cool. Reduce the remaining stock until it thickens and serve with the focaccia.

Stuffed Onions

Peel the onions and remove the tops and the stems so they will sit solidly in the baking dish. With a spoon, carefully hollow out the middles, leaving a shell. Bring the vegetable broth to a boil and blanch the onion shells for 5 minutes. Remove and place the shells in the baking dish. Reserve the broth in the pot.

Finely chop the insides of the onions and sauté with 2 tablespoons of olive oil for 5 minutes. Remove the onion and set aside. Cut the rolls and dried tomatoes into small cubes. Add the rolls and tomatoes to the pan with the remaining olive oil and roast this mixture for 8 to 10 minutes, stirring continuously. Remove from heat and stir in onions.

Preheat the convection oven to 340°F/170°C (for conventional oven: 375°F/190°C). Chop the Black Forest ham into small pieces. Wash the thyme, blot dry, and pluck the leaves from the stems. Sauté the ham and thyme briefly. Add the onion and tomato mixture and season with salt and pepper. Fill the onion shells with the onion, tomato, and ham mixture. Finely grate the parmesan and sprinkle across the tops. Pour ¾ cup + 4 teaspoons (200 ml) of the reserved vegetable broth to the baking dish and braise in the oven for 40 minutes.

4 large onions
4¼ cup (1 l) vegetable broth
5 tablespoons olive oil
2 day-old rolls
6 dried tomato filets
8 Black Forest ham slices
1 small bunch of thyme
Salt
Pepper
2 oz (50 g) parmesan cheese

ALSO:
1 baking dish

Makes 4 servings
Preparation time: 1 hour
Bake time: 40 minutes

Onion Pasta

4 onions
⅔ cup +1 tablespoon (100 g) flour
1¼ cup (300 ml) olive oil
Salt
Pepper
3 teaspoons capers
5 anchovies
1 small bunch of thyme
17½ oz (500 g) spaghetti
6 tablespoons premium olive oil
Fleur de Sel
⅔ cup (60 g) parmesan cheese,
    finely grated

Peel and slice the onions into half rings. Dredge in flour and shake off the excess. Fry the onions in batches in hot olive oil (340°F/170°C) until golden brown and crispy. Drain on paper towels and salt immediately.

Finely chop the capers and anchovies. Rinse the thyme, blot dry, and remove the leaves from the stems. Coarsely chop the onion rings and mix with the capers, anchovies, and thyme. Boil spaghetti in salted water until al dente. Drain, but reserve about ⅔ cup (150 ml) of the water. Mix the water with the olive oil and the spaghetti. Place the pasta on the plates and spoon the onion mixture on top. Season with Fleur de Sel and pepper. Sprinkle with grated parmesan.

Makes 4 servings
Preparation time: ca. 40 minutes

Index

About the photographer:
Oliver Brachat (BFF), an educated cook and pastry cook
was born in 1967. Since 1997, he has been an independent
food stylist, and since 2008, he has been a still life photographer with a focus on food in his independent studio in Düsseldorf. Brachat has worked for renowned magazines and in
the advertising world for various agencies and firms. He has
photographed numerous German and foreign cookbooks.
Upcoming publications for Hölker Verlag include: *Brot
genießen, Unsere Weihnachtsbäckerei* und *Sonne* im *Glas.*
www.oliverbrachat.com

About the author:
Tobias Rauschenberger is a chef of international experience, a
passionate food stylist, and a cookbook author. He lives and
works in Düsseldorf.
www.tobiasrauschenberger.com

A heartfelt thank you for the valuable cooperation and the excellent foodstuffs:
Thees family (Johannes, Christiane, Daniel, Eva), organic farmers in Willich
Naturlandhof Schmidt-Etold, Kevelaer
Fruit and Vegetable Schier in Düsseldorf

Photography: Oliver Brachat
Recipe development and cooking: Tobias Rauschenberger
Styling and props: Oliver Brachat
Photo assistance, styling, and organization: Steffi Neff
Other contributors: Martin Gentschow
Editor of German edition: Christin Gewecke
Layout and Text: Wilhelm Schäfer